PRINCEWILL LAGANG

Self-Care in Relationships: Balancing 'Me' and 'Us'

First published by PRINCEWILL LAGANG 2023

Copyright © 2023 by Princewill Lagang

All rights reserved. No part of this publication may be reproduced, stored or transmitted in any form or by any means, electronic, mechanical, photocopying, recording, scanning, or otherwise without written permission from the publisher. It is illegal to copy this book, post it to a website, or distribute it by any other means without permission.

Princewill Lagang asserts the moral right to be identified as the author of this work.

First edition

This book was professionally typeset on Reedsy.
Find out more at reedsy.com

Contents

1. Introduction — 1
2. Defining Self-Care — 4
3. The Interplay of 'Me' and 'Us' — 7
4. Nurturing Personal Well-Being — 10
5. Communication and Boundaries — 13
6. Recognizing Signs of Neglecting Self-Care — 16
7. Intentional Partner Support — 19
8. Quality Time and Alone Time — 22
9. Managing Stress and Conflict — 25
10. Self-Care Rituals for Couples — 28
11. Rejuvenating Romance and Intimacy — 31
12. Embracing the Journey — 34

1

Introduction

In the realm of modern relationships, the concept of self-care has emerged as a pivotal aspect that influences the dynamics between individuals. This chapter delves into the intricate interplay between self-care and relationships, highlighting the significance of prioritizing personal well-being while simultaneously fostering healthy partnerships.

Section 1.1: The Evolution of Relationships and Self-Care

The landscape of relationships has undergone a substantial transformation over the years. Traditionally, relationships were often perceived as entities in which two individuals merged their lives and identities. However, the contemporary perspective recognizes the value of maintaining one's individuality within a partnership. This shift has given rise to the recognition of self-care as a fundamental factor in the sustainability of relationships.

Section 1.2: Defining Self-Care in the Context of Relationships

To establish a common understanding, it is essential to define the concept of self-care within the context of relationships. Self-care encompasses a range of intentional activities and practices that individuals engage in to nurture their physical, emotional, and psychological well-being. When applied to relationships, self-care extends beyond individual concerns, influencing how individuals interact with their partners and maintain a healthy equilibrium between personal and shared experiences.

Section 1.3: The Importance of Individual Well-being

Maintaining a strong sense of individual well-being is not just a personal endeavor; it is a cornerstone of building and sustaining healthy relationships. When individuals prioritize self-care, they bring a higher level of emotional resilience, self-awareness, and contentment to their partnerships. This enables them to contribute positively and authentically, enhancing the overall quality of the relationship.

Section 1.4: Nurturing Partnerships Through Self-Care

The chapter further explores how self-care acts as a catalyst for nurturing partnerships. By engaging in self-care practices, individuals are better equipped to manage stress, communicate effectively, and address conflicts constructively. This, in turn, creates an environment where both partners can thrive individually and collectively, fostering a deeper connection and understanding between them.

Section 1.5: Structure of the Book

Before concluding the introduction, an overview of the book's structure is provided. Each subsequent chapter will delve into specific aspects of the relationship and self-care dynamic. Topics such as communication, emotional boundaries, shared self-care rituals, and managing responsibilities will be explored, offering practical insights and strategies for readers to apply in their own relationships.

In summary, this chapter serves as a foundation for understanding the intricate relationship between self-care and partnerships. By emphasizing the evolution of relationships, the definition of self-care within this context, and the pivotal role of individual well-being, readers are primed to explore the subsequent chapters that will delve deeper into the practices and strategies

INTRODUCTION

that empower individuals to navigate the delicate balance between self-care and relationships.

2

Defining Self-Care

In the pursuit of personal growth and maintaining healthy relationships, the concept of self-care emerges as a foundational principle. This chapter delves into the multifaceted definition of self-care, its profound impact on personal development, and the symbiotic relationship between self-care and the health of partnerships.

Section 2.1: Understanding Self-Care

Self-care encompasses a comprehensive range of practices and actions that individuals undertake to promote their physical, mental, and emotional well-being. It involves deliberately allocating time and energy to activities that nourish and rejuvenate the self. From engaging in relaxation techniques to pursuing hobbies and seeking solitude, self-care takes various forms tailored to an individual's needs and preferences.

Section 2.2: The Significance of Self-Care in Personal Growth

At its core, self-care is not merely a series of indulgent activities; it's an investment in personal growth. By prioritizing self-care, individuals cultivate a heightened sense of self-awareness, emotional regulation, and resilience. Engaging in activities that align with personal values and aspirations contributes to a deeper understanding of one's identity, fostering a positive relationship with oneself.

Section 2.3: Self-Care as a Foundation for Relationship Health

The connection between self-care and relationship health is intricate and profound. Individuals who practice self-care are better equipped to bring their best selves to their relationships. When partners prioritize their well-being, they reduce the likelihood of burnout, resentment, and emotional exhaustion, thus fostering an environment conducive to communication, empathy, and mutual support.

Section 2.4: A Balanced Approach to Self-Care in Relationships

While self-care is essential, it's crucial to strike a balance between individual well-being and partnership dynamics. Overindulgence in self-care at the expense of neglecting relationship responsibilities can lead to disconnect and misunderstanding. Conversely, neglecting self-care may result in emotional depletion that hinders the ability to contribute fully to a relationship. Striking a balance involves open communication, shared self-care rituals, and a mutual understanding of each partner's needs.

Section 2.5: Self-Care Practices for Relationship Enhancement

This section explores practical self-care practices that contribute to the enhancement of relationships. Activities such as maintaining personal boundaries, practicing active listening, and nurturing personal passions not only benefit the individual but also enrich the relationship by creating a foundation of mutual respect and admiration.

Section 2.6: Cultivating Self-Care Mindset in Relationships

Cultivating a self-care mindset within a relationship involves recognizing that individual well-being is not at odds with partnership health. Instead, it's a symbiotic relationship where self-care serves as the cornerstone for creating a thriving, harmonious partnership. By fostering a culture of empathy and understanding, partners can encourage each other's self-care journeys.

In conclusion, Chapter 2 provides an in-depth exploration of self-care's significance in personal growth and relationship health. By understanding the multifaceted nature of self-care, its role in nurturing personal development, and its profound impact on fostering strong partnerships, readers are better equipped to navigate the intricate balance between self-care and relationships in subsequent chapters.

3

The Interplay of 'Me' and 'Us'

Finding equilibrium between individual self-care and shared relationship care is a dynamic challenge that forms the cornerstone of healthy partnerships. Chapter 3 delves into the delicate interplay of 'me' and 'us', exploring the importance of striking a balance between personal well-being and nurturing the relationship, and highlighting how self-care enriches both partners and the relationship as a whole.

Section 3.1: Balancing Individual and Shared Care

Maintaining a balanced approach to self-care within a relationship requires a nuanced understanding of individual needs and collective responsibilities. Partners must recognize that nurturing their own well-being enhances their capacity to contribute positively to the partnership. Simultaneously, fostering a relationship care aspect involves joint efforts to create an environment of mutual support, communication, and shared experiences.

Section 3.2: The Power of Personal Fulfillment

When each partner engages in self-care to fulfill their individual needs, they bring a sense of contentment and confidence to the relationship. By pursuing personal passions, hobbies, and self-improvement, individuals infuse the partnership with fresh energy and enthusiasm. This personal fulfillment not only benefits the self but radiates positively into the relationship, promoting an environment of emotional abundance.

Section 3.3: A Cascade of Positive Effects

The benefits of self-care extend beyond the individual to ripple into the partnership. Partners who prioritize self-care experience reduced stress levels, improved emotional well-being, and increased self-awareness. This, in turn, enhances their capacity to communicate effectively, navigate conflicts, and offer unwavering support to one another. Thus, the relationship reaps the rewards of individual self-care practices.

Section 3.4: Strengthening the Bond Through Shared Care

While individual self-care is vital, shared care practices within a relationship are equally crucial. Engaging in shared activities that align with both partners' interests not only creates cherished memories but also fosters a deeper sense of connection. Whether it's embarking on joint hobbies, setting aside dedicated quality time, or engaging in acts of service, shared care cements the foundation of 'us'.

Section 3.5: Fostering Resilience and Adaptability

When both partners are committed to self-care and shared relationship care, they cultivate emotional resilience and adaptability. They are better equipped to weather life's challenges, support each other through transitions, and navigate the ebb and flow of circumstances. This synergy of personal and partnership well-being forms a robust shield against external stressors.

Section 3.6: Creating a Flourishing Partnership

The chapter concludes by emphasizing that the interplay of 'me' and 'us' is not a tug-of-war but a harmonious dance. Partners who understand the importance of self-care and shared care create a flourishing partnership built on mutual respect, empathy, and authentic connection. By nurturing their own well-being and actively tending to the relationship, they lay the groundwork for enduring happiness.

In summary, Chapter 3 delves into the intricate dynamics of balancing individual self-care and shared relationship care. By recognizing the power of personal fulfillment, understanding the positive cascade of effects, and fostering resilience through shared care, partners can navigate the delicate interplay of 'me' and 'us' to create a thriving, harmonious partnership.

4

Nurturing Personal Well-Being

Nurturing personal well-being is a cornerstone of maintaining a healthy and fulfilling life, which, in turn, contributes to the strength of relationships. Chapter 4 delves into the multifaceted dimensions of self-care, encompassing physical, emotional, and mental health. It also offers practical strategies for integrating self-care into daily life to promote personal growth and enhance relationship dynamics.

Section 4.1: Embracing Physical Self-Care

Physical self-care involves tending to the body's needs for nourishment, movement, and rest. Engaging in regular exercise, maintaining a balanced diet, and prioritizing sufficient sleep are essential components of physical well-being. By valuing and caring for one's physical health, individuals can boost energy levels, enhance mood, and cultivate a sense of vitality that positively impacts both personal life and relationships.

Section 4.2: Navigating Emotional Self-Care

Emotional self-care centers around acknowledging and nurturing one's emotional landscape. This involves practicing self-compassion, expressing emotions constructively, and engaging in activities that bring joy and fulfillment. By being attuned to emotional needs, individuals foster emotional resilience, which enables them to navigate relationship challenges with empathy and grace.

Section 4.3: Cultivating Mental Self-Care

Mental self-care focuses on nurturing cognitive well-being and maintaining mental clarity. This involves engaging in activities that stimulate the mind, such as reading, meditation, or engaging in creative pursuits. By taking steps to manage stress, reduce anxiety, and maintain mental equilibrium, individuals bolster their ability to communicate effectively and make sound decisions within relationships.

Section 4.4: Strategies for Integrating Self-Care

Integrating self-care into daily life requires intentional effort and planning. Strategies such as setting boundaries to prevent burnout, scheduling regular self-care activities, and learning to say no when necessary empower individuals to make self-care a consistent priority. Creating a self-care routine tailored to personal preferences and needs ensures that self-nurturing becomes an inherent part of one's lifestyle.

Section 4.5: Mindful Self-Care Practices

Mindful self-care involves being fully present and engaged in activities that promote well-being. Whether it's practicing mindfulness meditation, journaling, or engaging in solitary nature walks, these practices encourage self-reflection and self-discovery. Mindful self-care fosters a deeper connection with oneself, which, in turn, enhances the ability to connect authentically with others in relationships.

Section 4.6: Strengthening Relationships Through Personal Well-Being

Nurturing personal well-being has a transformative effect on relationships. Partners who prioritize self-care bring emotional stability, positivity, and a sense of fulfillment to their interactions. This enriches communication, deepens connection, and enhances the overall quality of the relationship.

Section 4.7: Self-Care as a Continuous Journey

The chapter concludes by emphasizing that self-care is not a one-time effort but a continuous journey. As individuals evolve, their self-care needs and preferences may change. Adapting self-care practices to align with shifting circumstances ensures that personal growth remains an ongoing process that contributes to the vitality of both individuals and their relationships.

In summary, Chapter 4 explores the dimensions of physical, emotional, and mental self-care and provides practical strategies for integrating self-care into daily life. By nurturing personal well-being, individuals enhance their capacity to contribute positively to relationships and create a nurturing environment for growth and connection.

5

Communication and Boundaries

Effective communication and the establishment of clear boundaries are fundamental pillars in maintaining healthy and thriving relationships. Chapter 5 delves into the vital role of open communication regarding self-care needs and the significance of setting and respecting boundaries to foster harmony within relationships.

Section 5.1: Open Communication About Self-Care Needs

Open and honest communication is crucial when discussing self-care needs within a relationship. Partners must feel comfortable expressing their individual requirements for personal well-being without fear of judgment or misunderstanding. Engaging in conversations about self-care preferences, routines, and the significance of certain activities creates a supportive environment where both partners can understand and respect each other's needs.

Section 5.2: Fostering Mutual Understanding

Effective communication about self-care allows partners to gain insight into each other's preferences and requirements. This understanding promotes empathy and a deeper connection, enabling partners to offer genuine support and encouragement for each other's self-care journeys. A willingness to listen and validate each other's needs strengthens the foundation of the relationship.

Section 5.3: Collaborative Self-Care Practices

Open communication opens the door for collaborative self-care practices. Partners can identify shared activities that align with their interests and needs, creating opportunities for quality time and mutual rejuvenation. Whether it's practicing meditation together, cooking healthy meals, or participating in outdoor adventures, collaborative self-care deepens the bond between partners.

Section 5.4: The Role of Boundaries in Relationship Harmony

Boundaries define the limits and expectations within a relationship, serving as a guide for respectful interactions. Establishing clear boundaries around self-care ensures that both partners understand each other's space, time, and needs. Respect for these boundaries fosters an atmosphere of trust, reducing potential conflicts and misunderstandings.

Section 5.5: Setting Self-Care Boundaries

Setting self-care boundaries involves communicating personal limits and requirements to ensure a healthy balance between personal time and shared responsibilities. Partners must express when they need solitude, relaxation, or engagement in certain activities. These boundaries allow for uninterrupted self-nurturing and prevent feelings of neglect or intrusion.

Section 5.6: Respecting Each Other's Boundaries

Respecting each other's boundaries is equally vital. Partners should honor the agreed-upon limits without judgment or attempts to infringe upon them. Demonstrating respect for boundaries shows a commitment to supporting each other's well-being and contributes to a harmonious atmosphere within the relationship.

Section 5.7: Strengthening Connection Through Communication and

Boundaries

By combining open communication about self-care needs with the establishment and respect of boundaries, partners strengthen their connection. The ability to communicate openly creates an environment of trust and understanding, while boundaries ensure that both individuals can engage in self-care without compromising the partnership.

Section 5.8: Embracing Growth and Adaptation

The chapter concludes by acknowledging that communication and boundary-setting are ongoing processes. As individuals and relationships evolve, self-care needs and preferences may change. Embracing growth and adaptation requires a commitment to continued dialogue and a willingness to adjust boundaries as necessary.

In summary, Chapter 5 underscores the pivotal role of communication and boundaries in maintaining healthy relationships. By openly discussing self-care needs, fostering mutual understanding, and respecting each other's boundaries, partners create a nurturing environment where personal well-being and relationship harmony coexist.

6

Recognizing Signs of Neglecting Self-Care

In the pursuit of nurturing relationships, individuals often find themselves inadvertently neglecting their own self-care needs. Chapter 6 delves into the subtle signs that indicate self-care may be taking a backseat in the pursuit of relationship goals. It also offers strategies for recognizing these signs and restoring the essential balance between personal well-being and relationship dynamics.

Section 6.1: Indicators of Neglected Self-Care

Neglecting self-care can manifest in various ways, affecting both the individual and the relationship. Signs may include increased stress levels, decreased emotional resilience, physical exhaustion, and a diminishing sense of personal identity. Partners may notice a decline in energy and enthusiasm, an imbalance between personal time and shared responsibilities, and an overall feeling of burnout.

Section 6.2: Emotional Disconnect and Discontent

When self-care is neglected, emotional disconnect may emerge within the relationship. Partners may find themselves becoming irritable, resentful, or emotionally distant. A lack of emotional fulfillment stemming from personal neglect can lead to strained communication and a diminished sense of intimacy.

Section 6.3: Overextending and Neglecting Boundaries

Overextending in the relationship while neglecting self-care can result in blurred boundaries. Partners may take on excessive responsibilities or compromise personal time, leading to feelings of overwhelm and resentment. This can ultimately strain the partnership and hinder open communication about self-care needs.

Section 6.4: Strategies for Addressing Neglected Self-Care

Recognizing the signs of neglected self-care is the first step toward restoring balance. Partners can engage in open and honest conversations about their feelings, acknowledging any imbalances and exploring ways to readjust priorities. It's essential to establish shared values regarding self-care and collaboratively create strategies for integrating it into the relationship.

Section 6.5: Reestablishing Personal Rituals

To restore equilibrium, individuals can revisit personal rituals and activities that promote self-care. Reengaging with hobbies, spending quality time alone, and pursuing passions revitalizes personal identity and emotional well-being. Partners can encourage and support each other in reestablishing these rituals.

Section 6.6: Seeking Professional Support

In cases of severe neglect of self-care, seeking professional support, such as counseling or therapy, can provide valuable guidance. A professional can help individuals navigate underlying issues, facilitate communication, and develop strategies to restore personal well-being and relationship harmony.

Section 6.7: The Continual Journey of Balance

The chapter concludes by emphasizing that maintaining the balance between self-care and relationships is an ongoing journey. As circumstances evolve, partners must remain attuned to the signs of neglect and promptly address them. Regular communication, self-reflection, and adaptability are essential to ensuring a harmonious interplay between personal growth and shared connection.

In summary, Chapter 6 explores the signs of neglected self-care and its impact on relationships. By recognizing indicators such as emotional disconnect and boundary issues, individuals can take proactive steps to address the imbalance and restore a healthy equilibrium. Through open communication, reestablishing personal rituals, and seeking professional assistance when needed, partners can navigate the delicate balance between nurturing personal well-being and fostering a thriving relationship.

7

Intentional Partner Support

Supporting each other's self-care routines is a cornerstone of nurturing a resilient and fulfilling relationship. Chapter 7 delves into the significance of intentional partner support, highlighting strategies for fostering a culture of encouragement and collaboration that enhances individual growth and contributes to the strength of the partnership.

Section 7.1: The Importance of Partner Support

Partner support plays a pivotal role in an individual's self-care journey. When partners actively support each other's well-being, they create an environment where personal growth is valued and celebrated. This not only enriches the individual experience but also strengthens the foundation of the relationship.

Section 7.2: Acknowledging Unique Self-Care Needs

Effective partner support begins with acknowledging that self-care needs are unique to each individual. Partners must take the time to understand and respect each other's preferences, routines, and activities that contribute to personal well-being. This understanding lays the groundwork for genuine encouragement and collaboration.

Section 7.3: Encouraging Personal Passions

Partners can actively encourage each other to pursue personal passions and interests. By expressing genuine interest, asking about progress, and celebrating achievements, they validate each other's journey and create a safe space to explore and develop individual hobbies.

Section 7.4: Collaborating on Shared Self-Care

Collaborative self-care practices can significantly enrich the partnership. Partners can identify activities that align with both of their interests and needs, fostering shared experiences that contribute to both individual and relationship well-being. Engaging in joint activities like cooking healthy meals, practicing meditation, or embarking on outdoor adventures strengthens the bond and promotes personal growth.

Section 7.5: Offering Emotional Support

Emotional support is a cornerstone of partner encouragement. Partners can actively listen, provide empathy, and offer reassurance during challenging times. By creating a judgment-free space for expressing feelings, they contribute to emotional well-being and fortify the relationship's emotional intimacy.

Section 7.6: Celebrating Milestones and Progress

Celebrating personal milestones and progress is an essential aspect of partner support. Partners can acknowledge achievements, no matter how small, with genuine enthusiasm. This celebration reinforces the value of personal growth and motivates both individuals to continue prioritizing self-care.

Section 7.7: Strengthening Connection Through Support

Intentional partner support strengthens the connection between individuals. By actively participating in each other's self-care routines and offering encouragement, partners demonstrate their commitment to growth and well-being. This shared commitment enhances communication, deepens understanding, and nurtures the foundation of the relationship.

Section 7.8: Mutual Growth and Enrichment

The chapter concludes by underscoring that intentional partner support is a two-way street. Just as partners offer encouragement, they also experience mutual growth and enrichment. By actively participating in each other's self-care journeys, they foster a culture of empathy, collaboration, and shared progress.

In summary, Chapter 7 explores the role of intentional partner support in nurturing self-care and relationship well-being. By acknowledging unique self-care needs, encouraging personal passions, collaborating on shared activities, offering emotional support, and celebrating milestones, partners create an environment where individual growth flourishes and the relationship thrives.

8

Quality Time and Alone Time

Balancing quality time as a couple and nurturing individual interests is a delicate dance that contributes to the harmony of relationships. Chapter 8 delves into the intricate interplay between spending meaningful moments together and valuing alone time. It also offers strategies for prioritizing alone time while maintaining a strong and healthy partnership.

Section 8.1: The Balance of Togetherness and Individuality

Balancing quality time and alone time is essential for fostering both personal growth and relationship vitality. Partners must recognize that while shared experiences strengthen bonds, maintaining individual interests and space is equally important. Striking this balance ensures that partners continue to grow as individuals while enhancing the quality of their togetherness.

Section 8.2: The Value of Quality Time

Quality time as a couple involves engaged, meaningful interactions that nurture the emotional connection. Partners can engage in activities that promote shared laughter, open communication, and the creation of cherished memories. Quality time strengthens the emotional bond and renews the sense of partnership.

Section 8.3: Nurturing Individual Interests

Nurturing individual interests is vital for personal well-being and growth. Partners must encourage each other to pursue passions and hobbies that align with their individual identities. By fostering a culture that values personal fulfillment, partners not only enhance their own happiness but also bring a renewed sense of enthusiasm to the relationship.

Section 8.4: Prioritizing Alone Time

Alone time is an essential aspect of self-care that allows individuals to recharge and reflect. Partners should prioritize regular periods of solitude to engage in activities that bring them joy, peace, and personal fulfillment. Alone time contributes to emotional resilience and allows partners to bring their best selves to the relationship.

Section 8.5: Communication About Alone Time

Open communication about the need for alone time is crucial for maintaining a healthy partnership. Partners should feel comfortable discussing their preferences and requirements for solitude. By setting expectations and understanding each other's needs, potential conflicts and misunderstandings can be minimized.

Section 8.6: Fostering Connection Through Balance

Balancing quality time and alone time fosters a deeper connection between partners. Quality time enhances emotional intimacy, while alone time promotes self-awareness and personal growth. Partners who respect and encourage each other's need for both experiences create a resilient relationship that thrives on mutual understanding.

Section 8.7: Establishing Rituals for Alone Time and Togetherness

Creating rituals for both alone time and togetherness provides structure to the balance. Partners can designate specific times for shared activities and individual pursuits. This approach ensures that both partners have dedicated opportunities for self-nurturing and partnership strengthening.

Section 8.8: Embracing the Dual Journey

The chapter concludes by emphasizing that the dual journey of quality time and alone time is a continuous process. As individuals evolve and circumstances change, the balance may need to be adjusted. Partners who navigate this journey with flexibility, empathy, and open communication continue to cultivate a dynamic and fulfilling relationship.

In summary, Chapter 8 explores the intricate balance between spending quality time as a couple and nurturing individual interests. By valuing both togetherness and alone time, partners enhance their emotional connection, promote personal growth, and create a relationship that thrives on mutual support and understanding.

9

Managing Stress and Conflict

Navigating stress and conflict is an inevitable aspect of any relationship. Chapter 9 delves into the transformative role of self-care practices in managing stress and conflict within partnerships. It explores how intentional self-care can enhance emotional resilience, offering practical techniques to foster a healthier approach to handling challenges.

Section 9.1: The Impact of Stress and Conflict

Stress and conflict are natural parts of any relationship, but their effects can be mitigated through strategic self-care. Unmanaged stress and unresolved conflicts can lead to emotional strain, communication breakdown, and a decline in relationship quality. Recognizing the significance of self-care in managing these challenges is essential for maintaining relationship harmony.

Section 9.2: Self-Care as Stress Management

Engaging in self-care practices is a proactive approach to managing stress. Individuals who prioritize self-care build emotional resilience, enabling them to navigate stressors with a more composed and grounded mindset. By practicing relaxation techniques, pursuing hobbies, and taking time to reflect, partners equip themselves to respond to stress in healthier ways.

Section 9.3: Self-Care for Conflict Resolution

Conflict resolution is facilitated by emotional regulation and effective communication, both of which can be enhanced through self-care. Engaging in activities that promote emotional well-being, such as journaling, meditation, or engaging in physical exercise, equips individuals with the tools to approach conflicts from a calmer and more empathetic standpoint.

Section 9.4: Techniques for Emotional Resilience

Emotional resilience is a key component of stress and conflict management. Partners can employ techniques such as mindfulness meditation, deep breathing exercises, and positive self-talk to cultivate emotional strength. These practices empower individuals to approach challenging situations with greater clarity and a heightened ability to manage emotions.

Section 9.5: Restorative Self-Care Practices

Restorative self-care practices are particularly valuable during times of stress or conflict. Taking breaks to engage in activities that provide comfort and rejuvenation, such as reading, taking a bath, or spending time in nature, enables individuals to reset their emotional state and approach challenges with renewed vigor.

Section 9.6: Open Communication as a Self-Care Tool

Communication is a foundational self-care tool when managing stress and conflict. Partners should openly communicate about their feelings, needs, and concerns, creating a safe space for discussing challenging topics. This practice not only fosters understanding but also prevents unresolved issues from escalating.

Section 9.7: Collaborative Conflict Resolution

Utilizing self-care practices to enhance emotional resilience paves the way for collaborative conflict resolution. Partners can approach conflicts with empathy, actively listening to each other's perspectives and seeking common ground. By valuing emotional well-being and effective communication, they navigate conflicts in ways that strengthen the relationship.

Section 9.8: The Ongoing Practice of Self-Care

The chapter concludes by emphasizing that self-care is an ongoing practice. Partners must consistently engage in self-nurturing activities to maintain emotional resilience and equip themselves to manage stress and conflict. By integrating self-care into their routine, they create a foundation of well-being that sustains the relationship through challenging times.

In summary, Chapter 9 explores the transformative power of self-care in managing stress and conflict. By prioritizing self-care practices that enhance emotional resilience, partners equip themselves to navigate challenges with greater composure and empathy. Through intentional self-care and open communication, they forge a path toward healthier stress management and more effective conflict resolution within the relationship.

10

Self-Care Rituals for Couples

Engaging in shared self-care rituals is a powerful way for couples to nurture their relationship while prioritizing their individual well-being. Chapter 10 delves into the world of collaborative self-care, exploring shared activities that strengthen the bond between partners and discussing the myriad benefits of participating in wellness practices together.

Section 10.1: The Essence of Shared Self-Care

Shared self-care rituals involve joint activities that contribute to both partners' well-being while fostering a deeper emotional connection. These rituals create opportunities for partners to align their interests, share experiences, and support each other's personal growth journeys.

Section 10.2: Exploring Shared Activities

Partners can explore a wide range of shared activities that promote self-care and relationship enrichment. Whether it's cooking nutritious meals together, practicing yoga, taking nature walks, or engaging in art, the possibilities are endless. The key is to choose activities that resonate with both partners' interests and enhance their bond.

Section 10.3: Enhancing Emotional Intimacy

Engaging in shared self-care rituals enhances emotional intimacy within the relationship. Partners share vulnerable experiences, creating opportunities for open conversations about personal feelings and aspirations. This deeper level of connection contributes to a sense of trust and unity.

Section 10.4: Fostering Mutual Support

Shared self-care rituals provide a platform for partners to actively support each other's well-being. Whether it's encouraging a partner during a challenging yoga pose or providing a listening ear during a joint meditation session, these acts of support strengthen the emotional foundation of the relationship.

Section 10.5: Encouraging Effective Communication

Participating in shared self-care activities requires effective communication and cooperation. Partners practice active listening, compromise, and understanding as they navigate these experiences together. This enhances communication skills that extend beyond self-care rituals into all aspects of the relationship.

Section 10.6: The Ripple Effect of Shared Practices

The benefits of shared self-care practices extend beyond the immediate experience. Partners carry the positive emotions and enhanced connection into other aspects of their relationship. The emotional nourishment gained from these rituals enriches daily interactions and creates a more harmonious partnership.

Section 10.7: The Joy of Shared Achievements

Accomplishing goals together during shared self-care rituals creates a sense of accomplishment and joy. Completing a challenging hike, mastering a new recipe, or achieving a shared fitness milestone enhances the sense of teamwork and achievement within the relationship.

Section 10.8: Sustaining a Culture of Wellness

The chapter concludes by emphasizing that shared self-care rituals contribute to a sustained culture of wellness within the relationship. By consistently engaging in these practices, partners cultivate an environment where individual growth and partnership vitality are equally valued.

In summary, Chapter 10 explores the realm of shared self-care rituals for couples. Through engaging in joint activities that promote well-being and connection, partners foster emotional intimacy, mutual support, and effective communication. By embracing shared self-care practices, couples not only enrich their relationship but also create a foundation of wellness that contributes to their ongoing happiness and growth.

11

Rejuvenating Romance and Intimacy

Maintaining a vibrant romantic connection is essential for the longevity and happiness of a relationship. Chapter 11 delves into the role of self-care in revitalizing romance and intimacy, exploring how intentional self-nurturing contributes to a deepened emotional bond. It also discusses strategies for integrating self-care into intimate moments to enhance the overall quality of the relationship.

Section 11.1: The Link Between Self-Care and Romance
Self-care serves as the foundation for nurturing romance and intimacy. When individuals prioritize their well-being, they bring a sense of confidence, positivity, and vitality to their romantic connection. This self-assuredness enhances attraction and contributes to a flourishing partnership.

Section 11.2: Fostering Self-Love for Enhanced Connection
Self-love is a crucial aspect of self-care that positively impacts romantic connection. Individuals who cultivate a positive relationship with themselves are better equipped to offer love and vulnerability to their partners. This self-love forms the bedrock upon which a deeper and more authentic romantic connection can be built.

Section 11.3: Infusing Intimacy with Mindful Self-Care

Intimate moments offer an excellent opportunity to integrate mindful self-care practices. Partners can engage in activities such as shared massages, sensory exploration, or mutual relaxation exercises. These practices heighten sensory awareness, deepen emotional connection, and enhance the quality of intimate experiences.

Section 11.4: Emotional Presence During Intimate Moments

Being emotionally present during intimate moments is a form of self-care that enriches romantic connection. Partners should focus on the present moment, silencing distractions, and engaging fully with their partner. This emotional presence fosters a deeper sense of intimacy and validates the importance of the connection.

Section 11.5: Communication and Vulnerability

Effective communication and vulnerability are integral to self-care and romantic connection. Partners should openly express their desires, boundaries, and preferences, creating an environment of mutual understanding and respect. This open dialogue enriches intimate moments and deepens the emotional bond.

Section 11.6: Creating Intimate Self-Care Rituals

Integrating self-care into intimate moments involves creating rituals that promote well-being and connection. Partners can engage in joint self-care activities, such as practicing synchronized breathing or taking turns giving and receiving nurturing gestures. These rituals enhance both individual and shared intimacy.

Section 11.7: Enhancing Sensuality Through Self-Care

Sensuality and self-care are intertwined. Engaging in practices that promote self-awareness and relaxation, such as meditation or mindful touch, can enhance the sensual experience within the relationship. Partners who prioritize self-care bring a heightened sense of sensuality to their romantic interactions.

Section 11.8: Cultivating a Lasting Romantic Connection

The chapter concludes by emphasizing that rejuvenating romance and intimacy is an ongoing effort. By integrating self-care practices into romantic interactions, partners create a lasting romantic connection built on mutual respect, vulnerability, and shared well-being.

In summary, Chapter 11 explores the role of self-care in revitalizing romance and intimacy. By fostering self-love, infusing mindful self-care into intimate moments, and prioritizing emotional presence and vulnerability, partners enhance the depth and quality of their romantic connection. Through intentional self-nurturing and the integration of self-care into intimate experiences, couples forge a path toward enduring romance and intimacy within their relationship.

12

Embracing the Journey

As the journey of balancing self-care and partnership unfolds, couples have the opportunity to create a harmonious and resilient relationship. Chapter 12 invites partners to reflect on their experiences, summarizes key takeaways, and offers guidance for nurturing a partnership that thrives on the interplay of personal growth and shared connection.

Section 12.1: Reflecting on the Balancing Act

The journey of balancing self-care and partnership is marked by growth, challenges, and deepened understanding. Partners should take time to reflect on their individual progress, the evolution of their relationship, and the impact of their self-care efforts. This reflection fosters gratitude and a renewed commitment to nurturing both personal well-being and partnership vitality.

Section 12.2: Celebrating Growth and Milestones

Celebrating personal growth milestones and relationship achievements is a way to honor the journey. Partners can acknowledge how far they've come, individually and as a couple, and appreciate the positive changes that have been fostered through intentional self-care and shared support.

Section 12.3: Key Takeaways and Lessons Learned

Summarizing key takeaways from the journey underscores the importance of self-care and shared partnership support. Partners should reflect on insights gained about effective communication, emotional resilience, and the balance between alone time and quality time. These lessons learned serve as valuable tools for future growth.

Section 12.4: Fostering Resilience in the Relationship

Guidance for fostering a resilient relationship revolves around continued commitment to self-care and partnership well-being. Partners should embrace open communication, actively support each other's self-care needs, and adapt self-nurturing practices as circumstances change. Resilience is nurtured through a willingness to evolve and grow together.

Section 12.5: Maintaining the Dual Focus

Sustaining a partnership built on self-care requires maintaining a dual focus on personal well-being and shared connection. Partners should continuously seek ways to balance quality time, alone time, and collaborative self-care rituals. This dual focus ensures that both individuals and the relationship continue to thrive.

Section 12.6: Nurturing a Culture of Positivity

Partners should foster a culture of positivity within the relationship. Expressing appreciation, offering encouragement, and celebrating each other's successes contribute to a nurturing environment where personal growth and shared well-being are highly valued.

Section 12.7: Embracing Change and Growth

The chapter concludes by emphasizing that change and growth are inevitable aspects of the journey. Partners should embrace the ebb and flow of life, remaining open to new self-care practices, shared experiences, and evolving dynamics. By embracing change, partners ensure that the journey remains dynamic and fulfilling.

In summary, Chapter 12 encourages partners to embrace the journey of balancing self-care and partnership. Through reflection, celebration of growth, and a commitment to continued well-being, couples can cultivate a resilient relationship that thrives on the synergy of personal growth and shared connection. By summarizing key takeaways and fostering a culture of positivity, partners lay the foundation for enduring happiness and harmony in their relationship.

Conclusion

The journey of exploring the delicate interplay between self-care and partnership has led us to a profound realization: the well-being of both individuals and relationships hinges on the intentional cultivation of personal growth and shared connection. Throughout this exploration, we've discovered that self-care is not a solitary endeavor but a powerful force that nurtures both the self and the partnership. As we conclude this journey, we reinforce the notion that prioritizing self-care is not only essential but transformative for both individuals and their relationships.

Self-care, often celebrated for its benefits on personal well-being, extends its reach into the realm of partnerships with remarkable impact. Through self-care, individuals bring emotional resilience, positivity, and a renewed sense of purpose to their relationships. They create an environment where open communication, vulnerability, and understanding flourish. This foundation paves the way for dynamic growth and a resilient partnership that navigates challenges with grace.

In the process of balancing self-care and partnership, we've explored how to maintain individual identity while nurturing shared connection. We've discussed the importance of open communication, the establishment of boundaries, and the power of intentional partner support. We've delved into the art of managing stress, resolving conflicts, and rejuvenating romance through self-care. Through shared self-care rituals and the integration of self-nurturing into intimate moments, we've witnessed how the relationship flourishes when nurtured by both individual and collective well-being.

As we bid farewell to this journey, we extend a heartfelt encouragement to you, dear readers. Embrace the idea that self-care is not a luxury but a necessity—a foundational pillar that sustains both personal growth and the partnership's vitality. Prioritize self-care as a conscious act of love for yourself and your partner. Recognize that by nourishing your individual well-being, you are, in turn, enriching the connection that binds you.

As you navigate the intricacies of self-care within your partnership, remember that the journey is ongoing. The ebb and flow of life will undoubtedly bring change, challenges, and new opportunities for growth. Embrace these moments with an open heart, armed with the knowledge that by prioritizing self-care, you are fostering a partnership that not only endures but thrives.

In this final reflection, we celebrate the transformative potential of self-care within relationships. May you carry the lessons learned on this journey into your lives, enriching your partnership with compassion, understanding, and the shared commitment to nurturing well-being. With each self-care choice you make, you contribute to a brighter, healthier, and more harmonious future for both yourself and your beloved partnership.

www.ingramcontent.com/pod-product-compliance
Lightning Source LLC
LaVergne TN
LVHW051926060526
838201LV00062B/4710